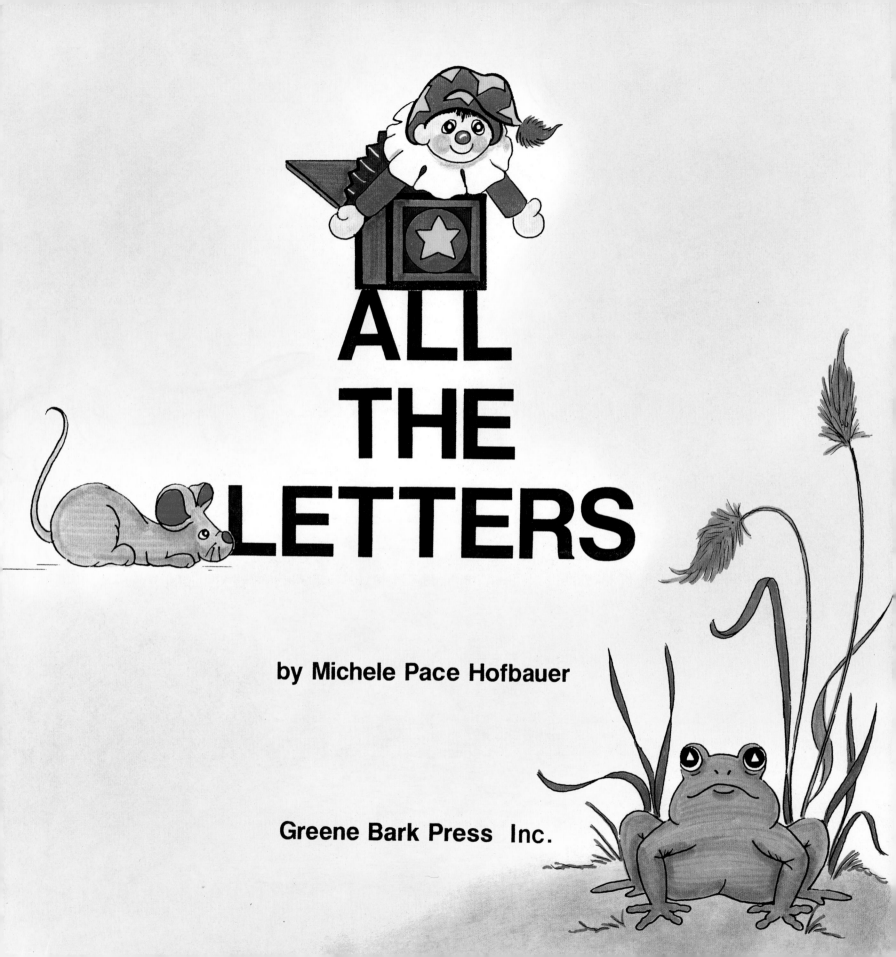

ALL
THE
LETTERS

by Michele Pace Hofbauer

Greene Bark Press Inc.

Dedicated to my son Michael

Text and Illustrations copyright © 1993 by Michele Pace Hofbauer
Second Printing March 2000
All Rights Reserved

Library of Congress Catalog #: 93-77607

Library of Congress Cataloging in Publication Data
Hofbauer, Michele Pace
All the Letters

Summary: An illustrated alphabet book specifically designed for
early learners. It serves as an introduction to letter, phonics,
object and color recognition.
1. Children's stories, American.   [1. Alphabet-Fiction]
I. Hofbauer   II. Title
Oct. 1993 (E)
ISBN 1-880851-08-3
Printed in Hong Kong
Published By:
Greene Bark Press Inc.,
P.O. Box 1108
Bridgeport, CT 06601-1108

ALL THE LETTERS

Aa

apple

acorns

anchor

airplane

Bb

balloons

butterfly

baseball

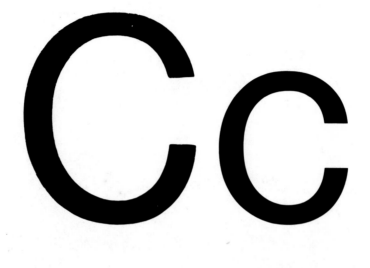

Cc

candycane

crayons

candle

carrot

caterpillar

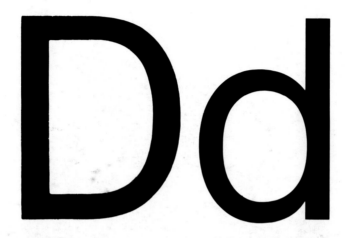

Dd

dinosaur

duck

dog

Ee

elephant

eggs

elf

F f

feather

flag

frog

fish

Gg

giraffe

grapes

green grass

hippopotamus

house

heart

hats

I i

ice cream

igloo

ink

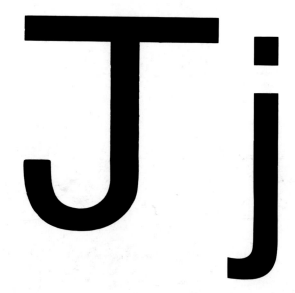

J j

jack-in-the-box

jellybeans

jumprope

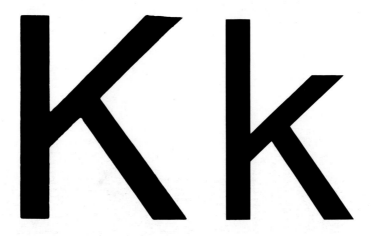

Kk

kangaroo

keys

kite

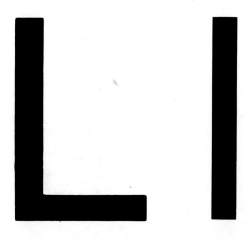

lollipops

ladybug

ladder

lion

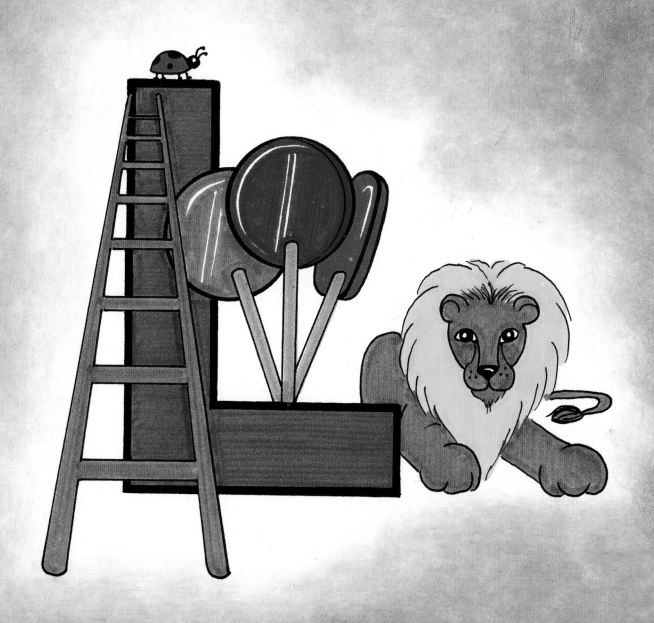

Mm

mushrooms

mouse

moon

Nn

nine nuts

nose

nails

nest

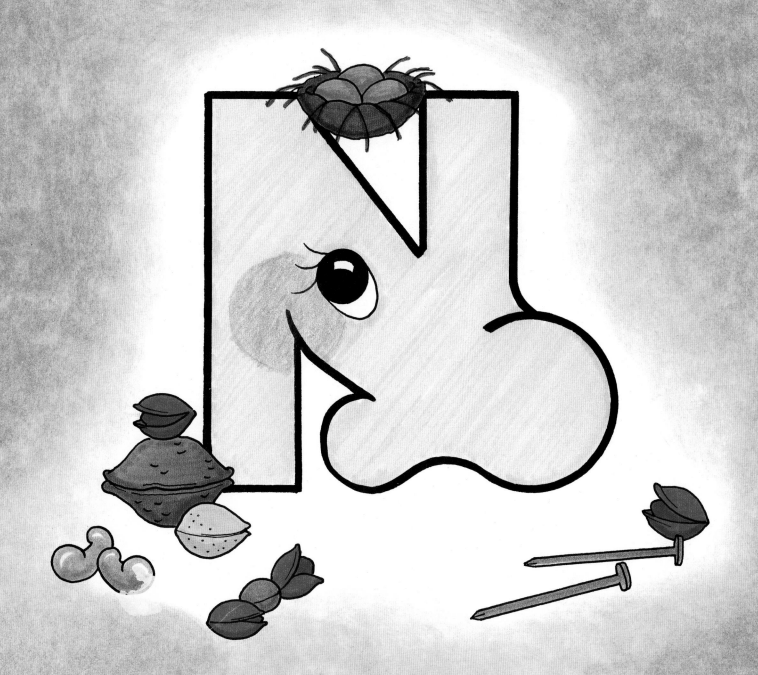

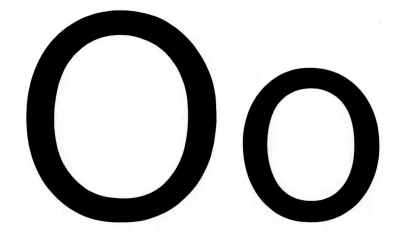

octopus

orange

owl

Pp

purple paint

paintbrush

pumpkin

pencil

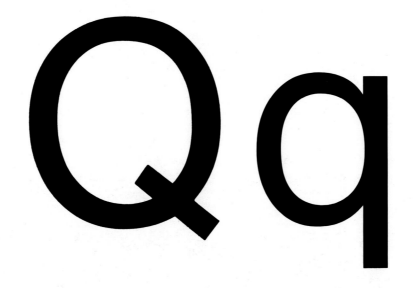

quilt

Rr

rabbit

Ss

six stars

sneaker

snake

sun

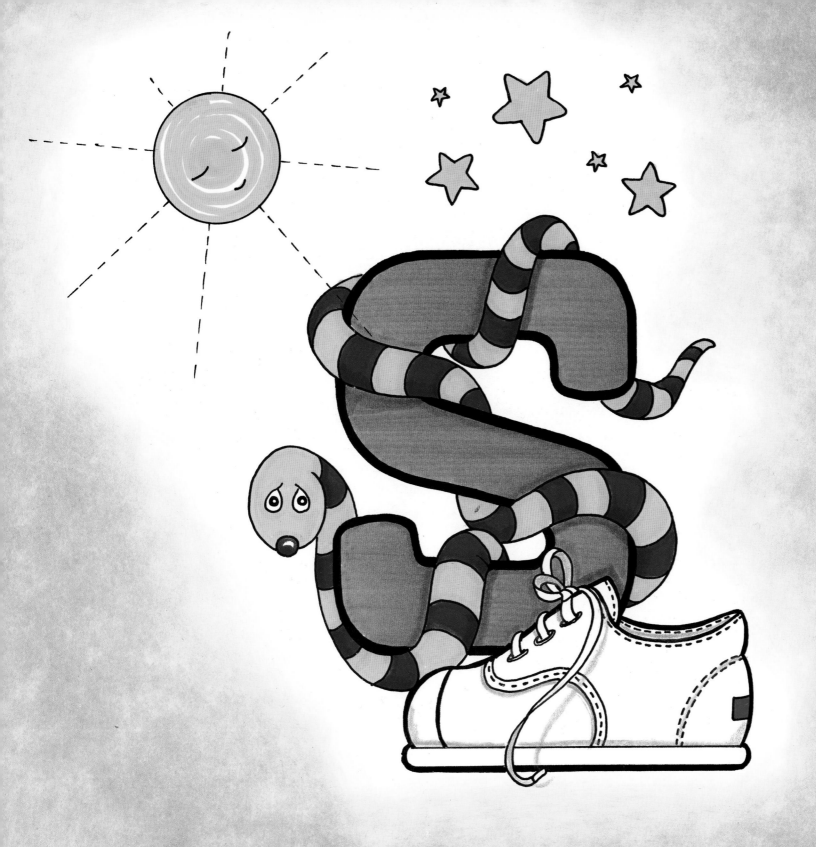

Tt

tulips

turtle

train

tree

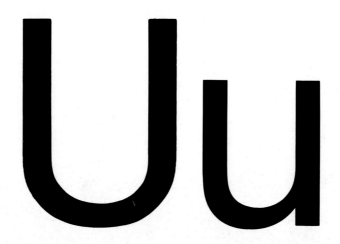

umbrella

unicorn

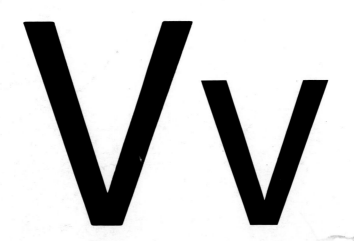

valentines

violets

Ww

windmill

wagon

worm

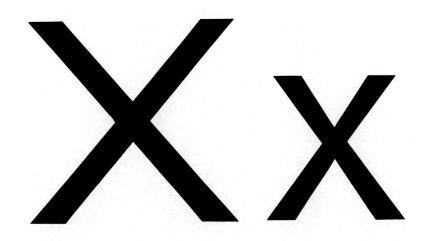

xylophone

xray

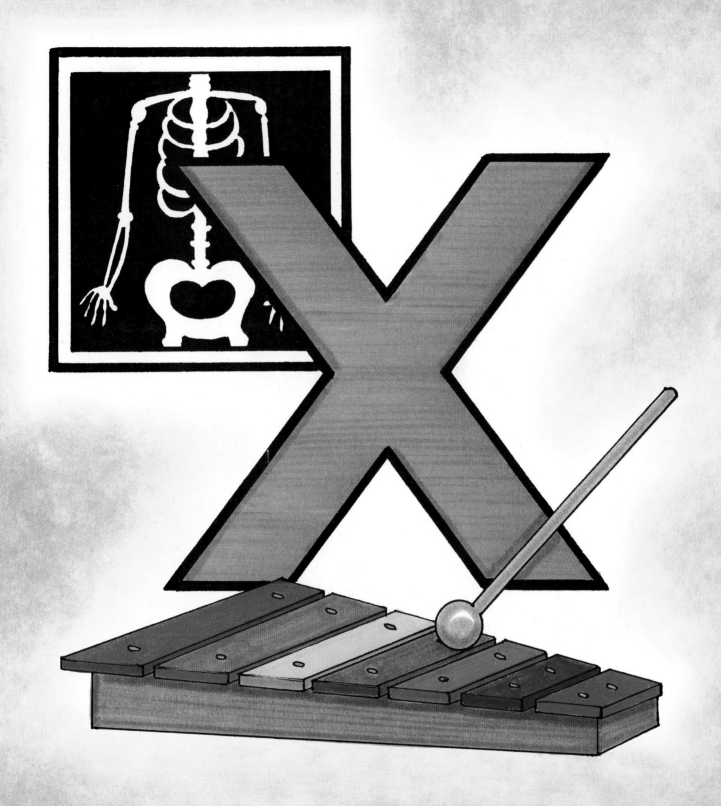

Yy

yellow

yo-yo

yarn

Zz

zebra

ALL THE LETTERS